KU-411-856

Athletics in Action – Track

David Hemery

Stanley Paul
London Melbourne Auckland Johannesburg

Stanley Paul & Co. Ltd

An imprint of Century Hutchinson Ltd
62–65 Chandos Place, London WC2N 4NW

Century Hutchinson Australia (Pty) Ltd
PO Box 496, 16–22 Church Street, Hawthorn,
Melbourne, Victoria 3122

Century Hutchinson New Zealand Limited
PO Box 40–086, Glenfield, Auckland 10

Century Hutchinson South Africa (Pty) Ltd
PO Box 337, Bergvlei 2012, South Africa

First published 1987

© David Hemery 1987

Set in Monophoto Times

Printed in Great Britain by Butler & Tanner Ltd
Frome and London

British Library Cataloguing in Publication Data

Hemery, David
  Athletics in action, track.
  1. Track-athletics
  I. Title
  796.4'26   GV1060.5

ISBN 0 09 166601 5

Contents

Acknowledgement

My thanks to Howard Payne for all the excellent photography in this book.

Introduction

The suggestions for training in this book are aimed at introductory level participants. It is assumed that those trying athletics are doing so for fun and for the challenge. Many young athletes, for example, will not want to train more than two or three times each week.

A slim book like this cannot provide a variety of schedules for different levels of training. So I am going to outline several different *types* of training for runners – the choice of what to do, and the frequency and the amount attempted will be a matter for each individual depending on event, age, maturity and desire.

Even though suggested workouts are included, it is preferable for an athlete to work with a coach rather than to work simply from a book. A good coach will help to balance a schedule according to the athlete's condition and progress. If youngsters would like to locate their nearest club or coach, they can contact one of these addresses.

Amateur Athletic Association
Francis House
Francis Street
London SW1P 1DL

Tel: 01-828 9326

Women's Amateur Athletic Association
Francis House
Francis Street
London SW1P 1DL

Tel: 01-828 4731

Every athlete will, at some time, be faced with the decision whether to make a serious commitment to hard training. It is recommended that the coach and athlete talk this through. Ultimately the athlete will decide when he or she is ready to push – and be pushed. A coach can be of great assistance in teaching, guiding, encouraging and, at times, acting as a conscience for the serious athlete. However, the decision to consistently push oneself should be made by the athlete, and only when the athlete is mature enough to be considering a long-term commitment. Starting too young, with intensity, creates a greater likelihood of both burnout and dropout.

Remember, sport should be enjoyed. Pushing, to move back the limits, can be enjoyable but it is different from playing. Most of those who have reached the very top in one sport played a variety of sports when young. Specialization often comes in the mid-teens. Taking part in a number of sports and a number of events has several benefits. To name three, it reduces the possibility of boredom, it allows the body to develop a variety of skills, abilities and muscular control, and it also allows the athletes time to discover the events they like best and the ones to which their more mature physiques are better suited.

Specializing in one sport or one event and pushing in training every day of the week, may produce rapid results when young, but it will often prompt the individual to stop playing long before they have reached their physical or mental peak. 'Little and often' is a valuable maxim.

If you do decide to train seriously, and do so five or six days every week, a very helpful rule of thumb is not to make more than two thirds of your sessions hard. The other one third should not be too demanding. They should be what are termed active recovery days. For a distance runner that might still mean a longish, steady run but at a gentle pace.

Planning your training

Although athletic events differ considerably in their requirements, the principles of conditioning remain the same. This is true whether the athlete is training throughout the year or whether limited to one term in the school year.

If the individual is completely unfit then a gradual progression of work is necessary. This route must also be taken when an athlete has had a couple of months off through injury. He or she may have to start by walking, swimming or cycling. The important aspect to remember is that the body needs time to adapt. The whole principle of training is that as you stress the body, it adjusts to the demands being made. You have a general idea of how gradually a body can change by seeing how it grows in childhood. There are dramatic changes but nobody's size and shape alters overnight. Patience and consistent work are the keys to success. If the process is rushed, the athlete can all too easily be hurt, sick or simply become fed up.

There are three basic ingredients which must not be ignored. The first is that the activities are seen as reasonably enjoyable, and that after each session the effort and activity can be viewed as worthwhile even if they never do lead to the desired aim such as a title. Setting

Sequence A
110 m hurdles
David Hemery

Sequence B
Sprint start
Eugene Gilkes

Sequence C
400 m hurdles on bend
David Hemery

Sequence D
Dip finish
Kathy Cook

9

challenging but attainable goals will greatly help the athlete.

The second is that the training must have helped to develop the skill level. Acquiring sound, fundamental skills is of vital importance. Under the stress of competition all individuals revert to what is second nature. If an athlete has repeated the best possible action a sufficient number of times for it to have become second nature, then under pressure the performance is less likely to fall apart.

The third ingredient is that the sportsman or woman must be allowed to decide for themselves when they are ready to make a commitment to *push* themselves. It is then, and only then, that the coach should assist by occasionally driving them to the difficult tasks which each know is necessary to reach full potential. Of course this kind of dedication need not be entered into until the athlete leaves school – or even later. There may be only half a dozen years in which athletes are willing to make sport their top priority and to work their bodies to match that interest. If they choose, or are encouraged, to push themselves too hard or too frequently when young then they will often quit long before they have reached their ultimate potential.

On average sprinters reach their peak in their mid-twenties, distance runners in their late twenties to early thirties and throwers up to their mid-thirties. There are exceptions to these figures on either
10

side of the age range, but this gives a guide to how long the athlete has to remain interested and motivated to improve. The key is to work on the first two elements – developing the necessary skills across a range of activities and enjoying the work and development.

Training emphasis

The concept of conditioning for better performance can be viewed as a gradual change of emphasis. Initially the concentration will be on a high volume of work. After a time the work volume will decrease and, almost in a direct relationship, the quality and intensity should increase.

Coaching principle

An important principle for the coach to hold is that an improvement in performance is just as high a priority as winning. The media in particular have done a great disservice by leading many to believe that anyone beneath first place is a loser.

Injury

It is a good rule of thumb that athletes will take about the same length of time to get back to fitness as they have had to take off. Thus taking four weeks off because of a twisted ankle will usually mean four weeks to get back to the level of fitness enjoyed before the injury. Do remember that most runners' injuries are stress induced.

What to do in training

It is important that every session involves a warm-up and warm-down. The warm-up should start with about five or six minutes' slow jogging. That usually means twice around a 400m track. This should allow the athlete to work up a very light sweat. This can be followed by stretching and sprint drills. Both are essential; the order is not important. Even distance runners will benefit from sprint drills as they help to develop the capability of moving faster.

The distance over which the drills are performed can vary considerably. I recommend that as part of a warm-up the minimum should be two sets each of As, Bs and Cs over 30m–40m (a separate section on sprint drills outlines how each drill – A, B and C – should be performed). The most important point to remember is that you are practising exaggerated but good sprint form. If you feel yourself rocking or leaning backwards, or some other non-sprint form, then you should try to correct it. Adopt the best sprint posture possible – running tall, on the balls of the feet, body straight and slightly forward.

Following jogging, stretching and drills it is normal for sprinters to run 2 × 100m, with a progressive build up of speed throughout the first 80m, then 20m easing down. This sequence is called strides, because it should open up the full stride and leg speed of the athlete.

Some distance runners like to do their strides and sprint drills following their distance run. It simulates the requirement to lift the knees at the end of an extended distance effort.

The remainder of training should be related to the requirements of the event and the overall plan for the year.

In a whole season's programme the first or background phase is to ensure general fitness and conditioning. In order to have a decent peak period, the base of a training 'pyramid' should be large and well established. Over the preparation phase towards competition the athlete should gradually change the emphasis from quantity to quality.

What follows is a look at different types of training which provide different pieces of the puzzle. It should be understood that each athlete has a different physiology. Thus training programmes may be similar, but it is important to discover what brings the best out of each athlete.

I believe that there is a spectrum of physiology similar to the spectrum which you find in nature. Sprinters are like paraffin: they explode and are burnt out in a matter of seconds. Middle-distance runners are like wood: they flame

13

for a time and many like to watch them burn. Marathoners are like coal: they glow for a couple of hours. Every athlete has the capability of working on becoming better in each of the other areas, but their basic muscle type is already genetically given. Sprinters may benefit from distance running, and distance runners may obtain value from weight training. There is a definite advantage in developing some ability; in each area. However, it is sensible to work mostly in the area of natural ability; the key to success is to find the best balance of work for the event requirements.

Background

Full-effort running can be very demanding on muscles and tendons. Therefore it is sensible to spend the first several weeks in preparation before embarking on full-speed running. The emphasis during this phase is endurance.

Endurance
Steady running

Sprinters may build up to 20–30 minutes of steady running. Distance runners of a young age may make an hour the ceiling. Once fully mature, the length of time may occasionally be as much as double those mentioned above. Although useful for sprinters, steady distance running is the staple diet for the long-distance runner throughout the training year.

14

The factors that vary are the distances and the pace. There is a belief now that although distance is necessary, more does not necessarily mean better. There is no doubt that in the background phase, long and slow distance is essential. But many distance runners are currently favouring quality over quantity. They have had years of training behind them, but it is worth noting that the year that John Walker broke 3:50 for the mile, and the year that Steve Cram ran 3:46, both had had injury problems which didn't allow them to cover great mileages. Steve said that his distance was all done at 5 minutes/mile pace! Obviously few athletes could handle that pace, but the point is that quality training with reduced volume seemed to provide the necessary format for top-class summer racing performance.

Fartlek (speedplay)

This involves a combination of jogging, running and fast striding. Usually a small group will take it in turns to site the next visible target and say, right we'll fast stride to the next park bench or telephone pole or to the top of the next hill. The tempo or speed should be lifted from a jog or run so that the athletes are lifting their knees and coming up off the balls of their feet. This is not a time to race. Where possible it is best to work with people of generally the same level of fitness and ability. This type of train-

ing session would be 30–40 minutes for sprinters and an hour for middle- and long-distance runners.

Long intervals

For sprinters a long-interval training session might be two or three runs over 500–800m. The rest period between each run should be sufficient to allow almost full recovery. The pace would be a good deal faster than the steady running. Gradually, throughout the preparation phase, the target times should be lowered. Recovery time is usually about the same distance walk as has been run.

Middle- and long-distance runners usually jog between long-interval runs. It makes a good deal of sense for distance runners to be varying the length of the intervals run. There is little point in doing 50×200m if the requirements of their event ask for longer concentration. A helpful rule of thumb would be to run at 80 per cent race pace. Thus, if you race at a 5 minutes/mile pace, add 20 per cent and train at a 6 minutes/mile pace for these intervals and work on a ladder, e.g. 600m – 800m – 1000m – 1200m – 1000m – 800m – 600m with a jog recovery of 2 minutes–$2\frac{1}{2}$ minutes–3 minutes–$3\frac{1}{2}$ minutes–3 minutes–$2\frac{1}{2}$ minutes. These recovery times would be for very fit, reasonably mature athletes. An extra minute or more on each recovery time might be necessary for the younger athlete.

16

Training provides stress and the body adapts. The adaptation takes place during the recovery time, both in training and between training sessions. The gradual transition to improvement is made either by gradually reducing the recovery time, say by ten seconds in each phase, or by increasing the pace of the runs, or both. These modifications should be introduced after the session has been run comfortably for a couple of weeks. For the middle- and long-distance runner it is more important to be working on reducing the recovery time than increasing the pace. The pace should be kept at a reasonably comfortable level. Inevitably, as athletes become fitter, they will be training at a slightly improving pace, but the main change is in gradually lessening the rest period.

Strength endurance

Sand-dune running

Those who live within striking distance of sand hills are very fortunate. They provide a type of strength and resistance training unmatched by any other surface. The effort should be explosive and maintained. Thirty minutes with a walk-down recovery between each hill run is the target. Allowing for a short recovery at the top, the target would be up to 12–20 × 10-second runs or 6–10 × 25-second runs.

Hills

After sand dunes, hills are the second

17

most beneficial tool for strength/power endurance training. Obviously hills will often be incorporated into distance runs, but the type of work referred to here is a specific session to run up and walk or jog back down. Sprinting uphill teaches the runner to lift the knees, to drive off hard and extend from the pushing foot. The arms are forced to work hard, and there is little likelihood of injury. Hill and sand-dune running should be done with intensity. Obviously the length and incline of hills vary. It is useful to seek out a variety which fulfil various training needs.

Strength

Weight training
Weight training is most commonly associated with strength development. That is its primary function and why it is mentioned here. However, it is also linked to training for endurance, speed and balance, and so is covered in more detail at the end of this training section.

Harness running

Harness running involves pulling a weight whilst running; it can be a very good strength exercise. The pulling cord should be 10m long, and the object may be a heavy tyre. A good type of harness is the one used by surf life-savers. The weights and equipment can be developed to suit the athlete.

Bounding

Although bounding is also listed under 'Drills' it provides enough strength quality to be worth mentioning separately in this section. One sprinter reached 20.2 for 200m using bounding as the major part of his training. As long as the action does not jar the legs too much, it can be an excellent type of training to greatly increase leg drive and power. It is not an exercise for a novice. Shin soreness (shin splints) can easily result from bounding.

Transition

During this relatively short phase the athlete is changing from the main emphasis on slower training to a greater emphasis on speed.

Slope

In this phase the most helpful terrain of all is a very smooth slope. I purposely chose the word 'slope' over 'hill' because running downhill usually means braking and probably leaning backwards slightly. Running down a slope is aimed to allow the athletes to move a little faster than they can on the flat. It enables them to extend their stride length more than they have been while running distance. The assistance to run faster than the body would naturally has an extremely helpful effect in the transition from steady-state running to

19

increasing the general tempo. A key way to get faster is to run fast; sprinting down a very slight incline is ideal.

Speed hills

Sprinting uphill at full speed and full effort provides another useful transition training session, as it is developing leg speed and strength with little likelihood of muscle pulls. The emphasis must be on faster leg speed than usually employed. The distance should be kept to what may be attacked explosively – about 5–15 seconds duration.

Speed

Speed endurance

100m sprinters, reach a peak of speed during their race, maintain it briefly, then begin to slow down. The athletes who look as if they are kicking away from the others at the end of a 100m race are merely slowing down less quickly! If slowing down is occurring in a race as short as that, then there is tremendous sense in working on speed endurance.

Obviously middle-distance runners spend most of their race time in a speed endurance context. Distance runners making a long break for home are experiencing the same requirements. The object is to run maintaining a constant fast pace throughout. In training the number of repetitions adds up to a total several times the distance of the track race. A 400m runner should run in training a total distance between 1000m and 2400m e.g. 10–20 × 100m, or 6–12 × 150m, or 5–10 × 200m, or 3–6 × 300m, or 3–5 × 400m, or 2–4 × 600m, or 2–3 × 800m. A full recovery should be made between each repetition, which may equal two laps' walk or about ten minutes.

Whistlers

This provides good practice at any time of the year for fast running without straining. The idea is to use the track beginning at the crown of the second bend. The athletes gather speed until they enter the home straight 'whistling', that is, moving as fast as they can without straining. They hold that pace for as long as they can without slowing but, as soon as they would have to strain to maintain that speed, they slow down and continue to walk around the track until they come to the start point again. The session may involve running 6–10 of these.

Short recovery

These sessions usually have a timed run and always a timed interval. It may be something as short as 30m to 60m sprints with 30 seconds recovery, doing 3–4 sets of 4–6 runs. It may be 2–3 sets of 2 × 300m with 1 minute recovery and 10 minutes between sets. Or it may be as intense as Seb Coe's 1200m, 800m, 600m and 400m, run in 2:51, 1:51, 1:18

and 49 seconds, with only 2 minutes recovery between each. These sessions really stretch the breathing, the body and the mind. Those reaching for their best must occasionally move into these high-stress sessions.

Top speed

Speed work should be over quite short distances (maximum 80m), and is performed with some intensity. A typical speed workout would be 6 × 40m starts, 6 × 60m flying starts and finish up with 2 × 120–150m. For sprinters some training over these short distances should be on the bend. This assists form and speed in 200m and relay races. Relay practices covering repeat runs over 50m makes a useful speed session.

Starts

Starting practice should be a part of a session at least once each week for sprinters. Sometimes this can be repeats over short distances of 20–30m or part of a ladder – up and down, e.g. 20m, 40m, 60m, 80m, 100m, 80m, 60m, 40m, 20m. It has been said that the only way to get faster is to run fast. Certainly that has some validity. It is also important to learn how to accelerate and run smoothly.

One helpful tip for sprinters is to picture that the body is already ahead and that you are racing to keep up with it. You don't want to be mentally dragging yourself around. Once you picture yourself running smoothly and fast you will keep up with that image.

Starting practice for distance runners is relatively rare, but there is quite a need to find a position which can be held with stability and from which it is possible to accelerate smoothly. I have found that placing the opposite hand on the knee of the leg which is up to the line provides good stability. If the other elbow is held back, flexed at right angles, but in the line of running, then the athlete is provided with a good chance of running away from the line with speed.

Speed ball

The Scots in particular place great faith in the use of the speed ball. This encourages rhythmic arm movements and develops endurance and strength. It has primarily been associated with boxers, but there is much to be commended in using it to promote concentration and coordination.

Weight training

There is a clear distinction between weight training and weightlifting. Lifting very heavy weights can damage young people. Weight training can be beneficial through the principle of specific muscle group overload, whereby the body adapts and strengthens when and where it is stressed.

23

The type of weight training varies with each part of the year. In the background or conditioning phase, the base of the pyramid, it involves many repetitions with light weights. If greater strength is being sought then there should be a transition to fewer repetitions but with heavier weights. It is the same principle as with running. The base of the pyramid is low intensity but high volume for endurance. Gradually there is a change of emphasis to high intensity and lower volume for more power and speed.

It is also important to keep muscle groups balanced. Therefore, for arm strength curls should be balanced with bench presses or pull downs. Sit-ups and leg lifts should be balanced with back arches. Step-ups and half squats must be balanced with hamstring curls.

There are a variety of weight-training exercises which can assist the development of endurance, strength and speed, but as long as arms, abdomen, back and legs are all worked the type of exercise depends upon the athlete's preference.

In the early phase, the amount of weight used should be approximately 60 per cent of maximum, working up from 1 to 3 sets, doing 8–10 repetitions of each exercise. If strength and power are wanted the transition is to 4 sets of 3–5 repetitions with 80 per cent of maximum.

For starting speed I recommend that

step-ups be done as if accelerating from the blocks. The back should be straight and the head up. The athlete should not try to spring off the foot on the ground, but take the body weight on the ball of the foot on the bench. The athlete should feel that all the work is being done by the thigh of the foot on the bench. The drive should be straight up, as if trying to drive the head through the ceiling. The amount of weight may increase, but the speed should be maintained with as rapid a drive up as possible. The weight may be on a bar across the shoulders, dumbbells, or a weight vest for the very young.

As arm speed determines leg speed, strong arms and shoulders are important to the sprinter and well-conditioned arms are vital to the distance runner.

Distance runners often avoid weights because this is not one of their strengths. However, if the arms are allowed to remain weak they will tire and slow down and the legs will follow. The old maxim that the chain is only as strong as its weakest link provides an important warning for those who ignore weights. Some distance runners might question the need for power in a middle- or long-distance athlete. It is interesting to note that during one training weekend for international distance runners on sand dunes in Wales, the fastest uphill times equated directly with the size of thigh muscles, so the larger the thigh muscle

25

on the distance runner, the faster they were up the dunes. Top of the list was Steve Ovett. The development of power is a valuable commodity and weight training can greatly assist the development of that power.

Tactical training

In a middle- or long-distance race one of the features which has to be covered is the break. At some point, one or other athlete is going to inject a change of pace and/or a 'break for home'. It is helpful to have a session which simulates this. If possible a group should be formed of similar ability. The athletes take it in turns to lead. An example of a session might be that the group are going to run 4–5 × 600m. The leader has the assignment to make a break for home somewhere in the last 300m to be determined by the leader. No one else may pass the leader before the jump is made. Obviously the following runners have the simulation of race conditions, trying to be in a good position and to avoid being boxed in before racing to the finish line.

For all races beyond 100m, judging pace is an essential part of preparation. Being able to judge pace accurately can be a very valuable asset. Athletes can learn to judge pace more easily if they repeatedly work with a watch. They should be challenged not only to assess the timed run, but to run an even pace to produce, say, a 30 second 200m or a 60 second 400m. Obviously, when running for pace, there should be a margin of comfort. By that I mean that if the athlete's best time for 400m is 58 seconds then there is little point in doing pace judgement work at 60 seconds. The effort to reach that time would be too close to maximum. The object in learning good pace judgement is to be able to spread the effort out over the race distance to produce the best result.

In-season specific training

Training during, and just prior to, the racing season should include sessions which relate quite specifically to the distance being raced. This is easier for the shorter-distance runners, but it is important at all distances. If the athlete is to race over 400m then the sessions should be just under and just over that distance. The over distance, 500–600m, is to keep in touch with the endurance base. The under distance, 250–350m, is run at race pace or better, to rehearse the requirements of speed and speed endurance.

Having listed many types of training, some of which are quite intense, it should be remembered how to reach a peak. The training should not be so intense that enthusiasm is lost. One rule of thumb is to have approximately two thirds of the training sessions hard, the other one third as active recovery.

Warming up

On a warm day athletes may be quite warm enough to feel comfortable, especially if they are wearing a track suit. The need to warm up may seem quite irrelevant. Why should they bother to jog to warm up when they are already warm?

The expression 'warm-up' can be quite misleading. The term refers to the preparation of the body and the mind for a certain level of work. Sometimes it can refer to *all* types of preparation which come under the general heading of training.

Warming up is obviously necessary on cold days. But even on hot days the interior of the muscle needs to be made loose.

A simple illustration of the purpose of warming up can be given by noting how difficult it is to open and close your hand, if you are not wearing gloves, on a cold day. Yet when your hand is warm you can open and close it almost faster than the eye can see. Jogging slowly, progressive stretching and other exercises all help to warm up the insides of the muscles. Similar to a car, performance and power are best achieved when the engine is warm.

28

Four important benefits can result from warming up properly.

1 *More speed* – It is possible to move faster, and all track and field events need speed.
2 *Less injury* – There is a tremendous reduction in the chance of injury if the athlete is well warmed up and properly stretched.
3 *Easier to train well* – Your performance in training or competition will be easier if you have fully and gradually prepared the system for a good effort.
4 *Strength and endurance* – The warm-up can make you stronger and fitter if it contains elements of strengthening and conditioning work.

The total length of time spent in the warming-up part of a workout may last anywhere from 15 to 50 minutes. Effort in the warm-up should be increased gradually and progressively.

As the warm-up is a part of the preparation for training and competition it is important that each athlete develops and maintains a consistent routine.

The warm-up is for the mind as well as the body. This is particularly true in the time before competition.

Each event will have some skill drills which should constitute part of the warm-up. Each athlete should gear his or her warm-up to the specific requirements of their event.

29

In addition there are certain general items which will be done by all. All running events will have a warm-up which includes jogging for at least five minutes. This should be done at a comparatively slow pace, and should be followed by stretching and drills, the main timed or effort-related activity and the warm-down.

The warm-down is very similar to the warm-up. It must include approximately 800m slow jogging and also stretching, as running tends to tighten and shorten muscles. Without stretching/flexibility work the athlete will be flirting with injury – as well as reducing fluidity and speed of performance.

Sprint drills

Sprinting action can be vastly improved with practice. One of the most helpful ways of modifying form, and thus assisting speed, is the use of sprint drills. Obviously the use of these is not limited to sprinters. All runners should derive considerable benefit in running faster and more smoothly through practising these drills.

'A'

The action of sprinting can be broken down into three phases. The first, referred to as 'A', is concentration on knee lift (see sequence E). For ballet the toes are pointed down; sprinters must practise the opposite. All practice should be done on the ball of the foot with the toe of the raised foot being lifted as high as possible. In all phases the arms approximate sprint form and hold the elbow close to right angles.

One common error is bending the supporting leg. It is important to practise staying tall and running tall. Another error is allowing the arm to open out on the way back. Considerable benefit will come from repeated correct motion being practised in the drills.

31

a

c

Bounding: learning to bound may be easiest across the track, trying to clear a lane with each stride. The drive should be out rather than up. The knee is driven to waist height, the arm punched to chin height, and both

b

d

are held for a second before landing and driving the other knee and arm up to the held position. The action should flow as much as possible.

The 'A' drills can include the following:

1 High knees – walking, jogging and running.

2 Skipping for height.

3 Bounding for distance.

'B'

The 'B' phase incorporates the high knee lift, but the emphasis is on extending the heel and pulling the leg to the ground (see sequence F). In this drill the most common error is that the athlete tends to allow the body to lean back while pushing the heel out or when drawing the foot down to the ground. This is where strong abdomen muscles will be important.

The 'B' drill – leg extension and pull down – may be applied to walking, jogging and running. The last is extremely demanding and requires some effort to maintain sprint form. This drill can also be done with a half-height foot lift and pull down for rapid leg speed action, i.e. extending the heel at 12–18 inches rather than 2–3 feet above the ground.

'C'

The 'C' phase is the recovery component. The athlete must remain in sprinting body position and, stepping rapidly, bring alternate heels up to the seat (see sequence G). It is the easiest, and arguably the most important, because it is working the hamstring muscle at the back of the thigh. Most of the sprinter's work strengthens the quadricep or front of the thigh muscles. Injuries occur most frequently when the muscles are in imbalance.

The 'C' drill – rapid heel to seat action – is best performed when jogging.

The walking drills of 'A's, 'B's and 'C's can be particularly useful when an athlete is slightly injured, e.g. when suffering from shin splints.

Drills may be done over varying distances. In the work done by their initiator Gerard Mach, 30m or less was the distance. I found that practice over longer distances was not only helping sprint form but was also developing excellent specific endurance.

Sprinting

Starting

The starting position must allow the athlete to move from stillness to top speed in the fastest possible way (see sequence B). In many cases the young athlete is not strong enough to benefit from a crouch start, although the standing start is unsteady for a sprinter wanting to race away from the line.

If athletes are taking a standing start it may be best for them to place one hand on the forward knee for balance.

The height and weight of sprinters varies considerably. This means that the athlete using a crouch start must discover the best personal starting position. Positions can be divided into three main categories: short, medium and long.

The front block is closest to the line with the short start, being one foot-length back from the start line. The rear block in the short start is another foot-length back.

For the medium start the front block is two foot-lengths from the start line, the rear block being again about a further foot-length back.

The long start has the front block two

36

and a half to three foot-lengths from the line, with the rear block a further foot-length back. This is the most difficult position for the beginner as so much leg drive is required to accelerate from such an elongated position.

Before the start the athletes stand behind their blocks. On the command 'Take your marks' they move forward. They usually place their fingers on the track for balance before backing into the blocks. They take most of their weight on the knee of the back leg and on their fingers. The arms are placed about shoulder width apart. The fingers are placed up to, but not on, the line and they are arched to make a tunnel effect. This is to raise the upper body as much as possible. The eyes are usually focused on the track a little ahead of the start line. When pressing the feet onto the block pad, the athletes must ensure that their toes are still in contact with the ground. It is not permitted to have the feet above ground level.

Once everyone is settled into their starting position the starter gives the command 'Set'. The sprinters have to be motionless in the set position before the starter will fire the gun. This is not an easy position to hold steadily for any length of time. The hips should be raised slightly higher than the shoulders and held there. A frequently seen fault is for sprinters to lower their hips while trying to stay set.

Kathy Cook on her mark, supporting her weight mostly on one knee and her hands. The hands are placed up to but not on the line, with the fingers making an arch. Her hands are a little more than shoulder width apart

In order to get the fastest start athletes should hold most of their body weight on their fingers. The shoulders should be moved forward so that they are over the start line. If the rear leg is straight in the set position then the rear block is too far back. Both legs must be in a position which allows for a strong push from the blocks.

If the athletes are in a crouch start position it is vital that they move their hands first, immediately the gun has

In the 'set' position the seat is raised slightly higher than the shoulders. The body weight is shifted more onto the hands, and the shoulders are moved forward over the start line

sounded. If they do not do this, and the rear foot is moved first, the athlete stands up on the first stride out of the blocks and loses the forward thrust. If the hands are moved first the legs must push hard to keep the body from falling over. This forces the athlete to drive hard with the legs.

Because a good set position is not easy to hold for long, it must be practised. This develops the required arm and finger strength and, of course, gives the athlete the opportunity to find the best starting position.

Block placement

The block position for 200m and 400m

39

is different from the straight dash races. In the 100m the blocks should be in the middle of the lane, pointing straight down the centre. In the longer sprints and relays the races begin at the start of a bend. The shortest distance around the curve is on the inside edge of each lane. It makes sense to run as close to the inside lane line as possible without actually stepping on or over the line.

European sprint champion Linford Christie, passing the athlete in the lane outside him. Linford could be a foot closer to his inside lane line. Both athletes are leaning into the turn, which allows them to maintain their speed while running around the bend

In order to set up the furthest straight run into that curve the blocks are placed towards the outside of the lane and aimed at the tangent of the inside lane line. The best way to see that the blocks are aimed correctly on the straight, and on the bend, is to move back a few paces and crouch down to see how well they are directed. When in the blocks at this angle in the 200m and 400m the athlete will have only one hand up to the line. As with the 100m start the hands should be about shoulder width apart, dropped straight down. This will mean the right hand is up to the line, but the left slightly back from the line. Both hands must be within the assigned lane.

Acceleration

The first step from the blocks should not be too long or the result will be a leg position from which it will be difficult to continue to drive hard and also it will raise the upper body too fast, causing a standing and stopping effect.

In the acceleration phase, which is at least 30m–40m, the body lean should be sufficiently pronounced that the leg drive is being effectively used. During the acceleration to full speed the body lean gradually reduces to an angle only slightly forward of upright. According to measurements of the world's best sprinters they reach their top speed after about five or six seconds. It is vital to retain concentration throughout the

41

race, and to think 'faster looser' rather than struggle. Relaxed muscles are able to move faster than tense ones.

One of the most valuable strength exercises to help start speed is step-ups. This is explained in the section on weight training.

Arm action

From the start the sprinter's elbow bend should remain close to right angles. The hand should not rise above about shoulder height and should not move across the centre line of the body.

An athlete's arm speed determines the leg speed. Many top sprinters are using the speed ball in order to develop the capacity to sustain a rapid and strong arm action.

While running the bend the action of the left leg and left arm is slightly shorter than that of the right.

Finish

The finish of a sprint race is often close, and the forward lean or 'dip' can make the difference of at least a body width – and this can mean a place or two. The dip should take place in the stride before the finish line so that the body is leaning through the line (see sequence D).

In all practices the athlete should be running past the finish line. A dropped effort when approaching the line often costs a place . . . and 'as you practice so will you race'.

Pace judgement in 400m

Because the 400m is a very long sprint it is important to spread the effort out as evenly as possible. The top 400m runners, in peak form, run the first 200m within about one second of their best 200m time and the second 200m with less than two seconds slow down. Some of the best times of all have been run when the athlete has managed to run both halves between even paced and $1\frac{1}{2}$ seconds difference.

As it is not possible to run 400m with the same all-out intensity of 100m it is necessary to practise running fast with the minimum effort. The race can be broken down into two 200m segments, four 100m segments or eight 50m segments. For this illustration of pace judgement it is most helpful to think of the race in four parts.

The first 100m should be run at about 90 per cent effort. This is when the tempo is established for the race. The second 100m is as fast as the first, but is the most important part in which to control tension. The pressure of acceleration should be relaxed and as much energy conserved as possible without any great loss of speed. This is often referred to as 'floating'. A useful way of checking on tension is to feel whether the hands, arms, neck or chin are tight. If all of these are relaxed then the athlete is a long way towards relaxed running. On the other hand the last thing needed

43

is for the hands and arms to go floppy! Usually the fingers are held in a slight curve with thumb on top of the first finger. The third 100m is another critical part of the race as there is a tendency to slow a little while running the second bend. Concentration should be high and thought should be on building effort throughout the bend. A good third 100m will set up the best possible time. The last 100m is a matter of maintaining sprint form – continuing to drive off the toes and using a good sprint arm action. This is where the speed endurance training and sprint drills pay off.

Relays

The relay event can be the most exciting in athletics. It is the only team contest of this very individualistic sport. The two distances over which most relay competitions are run are 400m and 1600m.

In principle, each athlete runs the same distance: 100m in the sprint relay and 400m in the longer relay. Different changeover patterns mean, in practice, that some runners may run further than others.

The object is to get the baton around the distance in the quickest possible time. With that as the aim, a most important aspect to practise is the smooth, rapid transition from one runner to the next.

4 × 100m

The 4 × 100m has a runner for each bend and one for each straight. Some athletes are naturally better than others at running bends. This must be born in mind when a team is put together.

It is also significant that there are some runners who find it difficult to

45

either give the baton or receive it. These factors may also have an influence on the running order as the lead-off athlete doesn't have to receive the baton and the last runner, the anchor leg, doesn't have to pass it.

Normally the best starter and a good bend runner is put on the first leg. The second and fourth legs are on the straight and there is advantage in using strong sprinters on these legs to take advantage of the potentially longer straight runs. If the baton is taken early in the exchange zone and handed over late in the next exchange zone the athlete on the second leg can carry the baton for the longest part of the 400m race. The third runner must be a good bend runner, but not necessarily the best starter. The argument for placing your best athlete last is that the competitive instinct in the champion sprinter will be realized to its greatest extent in a close finish at the end of the race.

In the sprint relay it is best not to change the baton from one hand to the other. It is also imperative that the bend runners run close to the inside of their lane so that they are not running further than absolutely necessary. With these facts in mind the lead-off runner should carry the baton in the right hand. The second runner must start and stay close to the outside of the lane and carry the baton in the left hand. The baton is passed to the right hand of the third runner who starts and stays on the inside of the second bend. And the final runner starts on the outside of the lane and receives and carries the baton in the left hand.

The baton exchange must be practised a great many times. Familiarity is vital, each runner knowing how they will pass the baton and how they will receive it.

There are two main choices.

The downsweep

The method I favour is placing the baton down onto the palm of the outgoing runner. The outgoing runner holds his or her arm straight back slightly above waist height, with the palm of the hand facing the sky, and the thumb held wide, parallel with the back. My reason for favouring the downsweep method of baton exchange is that at each exchange at least half of the baton is available for placing and grasping. A second advantage is that a slightly fuller stretch is possible and thereby more distance saved.

The upsweep

The second option is for the lead-off runner to hold the baton at one end with the majority of the stick showing. Each subsequent runner takes the baton slightly further forward on the length. The passing technique is for the incoming runner to use an upsweeping motion.

47

The incoming runner brings the baton down onto the open hand of the outgoing runner

The incoming runner brings the baton up, with his or her hand as close as possible to the hand of the outgoing runner

48

49

There are arguments for and against each method, but both techniques are used at international level.

Exchange practice

Exchange practice is needed most to determine the 'check point'. This is the point which the incoming runner passes to set off the outgoing runner. This is sometimes referred to as the 'go' mark. The object is to exchange the baton while travelling at equal speed. This means that the outgoing runner is given two or three seconds to accelerate up to the pace of the incoming runner. As the incoming runner passes the mark the outgoing runner sets off. This 'go' mark is usually around 15–25 foot-lengths from where the outgoing runner is starting. It may require more than this distance if the athlete is young and does not have a fast starting capability. Nevertheless the exchange should be aimed to be completed before the athletes are within the last few metres of the exchange zone. The check mark is made on a cinder track simply by scratching a line on the track. On an all-weather surface either chalk or adhesive tape may be used.

Starting for outgoing runner

It is essential to repeatedly practise starting from the chosen outgoing starting position. This is usually from a position of only having one hand on the track in the set position as the athlete is looking under the lifted inside arm to see the incoming runner reach the check mark. From that point on the outgoing runner should neither have to look back nor slow down. The outgoing runner must start consistently and not only stay on balance but also leave at least one third of the lane free for the incoming runner. Ideally the relay runners should never overlap, but it is essential that the incoming runner is never running directly behind the receiving runner. All too easily legs or feet can clash. There is also the requirement to stay within the lane. Straying, even one centimetre, into an adjacent lane can result in disqualification.

When starting to run, normal sprint form should be used. The receiving hand should come back only on the agreed signal call of the incoming runner. The hand should then move into the receiving position, held as steadily as possible. The transfer should take place over 2–3m. In perfect circumstances the pass will be at full arm's length for both athletes, the outgoing runner having reached the speed of the incoming runner.

4 × 400m

In this longer relay it is essential to always have a visual pass. The incoming runners are often close to exhaustion and therefore not capable of any change of pace to assist the outgoing exchange.

51

Their sole responsibility is to hold the baton out in their right hand, as steadily as possible, horizontally at waist height. The responsibility is therefore entirely on the fresh, outgoing runner to take the baton. The outgoing runner takes the baton with the left hand, to be switched to the right hand as soon as possible.

It is very important that the outgoing runner is facing towards the inside of the track. This is true for two good reasons. First, the athlete who does not face in has no guideline of the inside curve and may drift towards the outside of the track when receiving the baton. As the outgoing runner should be moving in to take advantage of the inside of the bend it makes sense to drift that way if one has to drift at all. Second, by facing the infield the runner's back can be used as a protection against crowding and against the accidental knocking of the baton during the exchange. Crowding often happens when a number of teams are in a close race; as the incoming runners come towards the end of their 400m leg the anticipation builds in the outgoing runners and the inclination is to press in towards the inside lanes.

There are no lane divisions after the first exchange so positioning is determined by the finishing order of the runners (the leading team on the inside, the second team next and so on). Added problems occur if several position changes occur within the finishing straight. If change occurs very late in the home straight it is best to stay where the incoming runner is aiming, as often they are running themselves out and they should not have to switch direction at the last minute.

Eugene Gilkes passes to David Hemery. Note that the incoming runner in the 4 × 400m relay extends and holds the baton at close to waist height. It is the responsibility of the outgoing runner to take it. The outgoing runner's legs are facing forwards but his upper half is turned sufficiently towards the infield to see the incoming runner. The focus must remain on the baton until it is safely in the hand. The baton is then immediately transferred into the right hand

b

d

54

c

e

55

Starting position

The starting position for the outgoing runner should be a half-turn of the upper body. The feet should be positioned to allow the athlete to run forward. The left foot backs close to but not over the relay zone start line.

Because the pass is visual and the incoming runner is not moving at top speed, the outgoing runner can afford to leave the start later than the sprint start but with speed once the time is right. Exchanges for this relay are all too often neglected and there is great merit in practising.

The hand position for the outgoing runner may be with the palm up or palm down. That can be determined with practice. I personally favour the fresh, outgoing runner having the responsibility of grasping the baton. The incoming runner must simply extend it parallel with the ground at about waist height.

4 × 400m Exchange zone rules

The exchange must take place within the 20m zone. The outgoing runner must start with feet within the zone. The baton must be released from the grip of the incoming runner before the line indicating the end of the zone.

The 400m time for each relay runner is taken as the baton crosses the start-/finish line, not from the point of exchange.

If the baton is dropped the athlete who dropped it must be the one to pick it up and pass it on. In doing this they must not impede other runners.

Middle- and long-distance events

It is recommended by most doctors and coaches that young people who are still growing should neither take part in long races, nor pursue intense endurance training. Such activities can retard normal growth and cause problems in bone development, particularly where heavy mileage is undertaken on hard surfaces.

It has been possible for children of less than ten years old to complete a marathon, but what is the point if it means that the bones of that child become malformed, or they suffer from unnecessary joint problems when they are older.

Most good coaches advise that pre-teenagers enjoy their sport. Intense and high-volume training is only introduced gradually as the youngsters are nearing full maturity. Enjoyment is the key to long-term fulfilment in sport. It has also been long recognized that there is a great advantage in developing speed when young. Most athletes move up in distance as they mature.

It is also important to point out that it takes many years to fulfil potential in distance running. This is because only a moderate improvement in time can be achieved by improved running technique. The majority of improvement for the distance runner will come through greater efficiency in using the oxygen taken in while running. The body modifies itself extremely slowly, probably at about the same rate that it grows. That means that the training should gradually and progressively introduce slightly more stress on the system.

Movement and posture

Each individual has a uniqueness of movement, part formed through their physique at birth and part developed through their childhood activities. The action can be improved through sprint drills which are now used by many middle- and long-distance runners.

Although there is little conscious technique involved in distance running, the beginner should recognize that the knee lift is much less than in sprinting. The arm action is also less vigorous and, instead of the arms primarily moving up and down as in the sprint, they gently move in balance with the legs, with the lower arm moving almost parallel with the ground and the hand moving to approximately the mid-line of the body, not beyond. Only when accelerating do the arms move into the sprint action, still at approximately right angles, but with the hands lifted up towards chin

59

height. The hand at this time should be moving between the waist and chin level half way between the mid-line and the shoulder. The hands should not be clenched, but the fingers are usually curled with the thumb on top (see sequence H).

There should be as much relaxation as possible while still maintaining control. Unnecessary physical or mental tension during a race can drain the athlete.

Pace judgement and tactics

The object of racing is to compete with others, usually racing fast. There is no point in entering races beyond one's level and becoming immediately disillusioned by results. It is best to choose a level where one is in with a chance of being reasonably competitive. That does not mean that it's necessary to win every time out. What is important is the need to be able to race competitively and learn from each experience. In this way athletes realize that fitness is not the only aspect of racing; they begin to recognize the importance of tactics. The athlete must run with awareness, not only of their own feelings and thoughts but also of the intention and actions of others in a race.

In the shorter middle-distance races the start is more important than in long-distance races. In the first 200–300m the runners establish their preferred position in the race. A small number enjoy front running. They dictate the pace for the whole field and, to some extent, control the race by the pace they choose to establish. Behind the leader there is frequently a battle for the position on the leader's shoulder. This position is preferred by most as it does not have the pressures of leading but is the perfect position to make a challenge for the lead or to cover the challenge of any other runner advancing from the rear.

A common problem is trying to avoid being boxed in. This situation can occur when the athlete has chosen to run close to the inside of the track and thereby runs the shortest distance (each lane out adds approximately 8m to the distance covered each lap). It's a compromise because if the athlete is following the leader and a file of runners comes past the leader, the athlete directly behind a tired leader will often have to wait for the whole field of runners to pass before he or she has the opportunity to pull out and pass. The rules state that an athlete must not impede the progress of another competitor. That means that athletes may be disqualified if they either push their way out or step out in front of another athlete without being a clear stride or two ahead.

Passing on a bend is not generally recommended. It has an added element of surprise, but that advantage is considerably offset by the extra distance

61

covered by running wide on a bend. Passing may have to take place on a bend if the lead runner's pace is sagging or if there is a break (sudden increase of pace) up front. The athlete running 'in the pack' must always be conscious of this, and must decide whether to cover the break (go with the new pace) or not. If the athletes at the front are all moving past the leader it is essential to go too if you have any intention of winning.

Only practice can establish when each athlete can and should strike for home. Starting a kick from too far out and slowing dramatically before the finish line can lose several places. Conversely the advantage of making an early attack improves the element of surprise. It also means that the opponents have to make an instant decision as to whether they are prepared to risk their own chances by trying to match an early effort. International athletes like Brendan Foster and Dave Bedford used to throw in a dramatic change of pace in the middle part of a long race. They usually succeeded in breaking away from the main group and established dominance by maintaining, and occasionally increasing, their commanding lead. Marathoners Joan Benoit Samuelson in the 1984 Olympics and Rob de Castella in the 1986 Commonwealth Games made their breaks so early that no one else followed. It takes courage, confidence, commitment and concentration to

62

attempt such a move in any distance race, but particularly in a marathon.

Effort distribution

In many races the athletes who attempt to cover every move with an explosive counterattack find that they are lacking at the finish. It is preferable to make only one major change of pace effort during a race. This may not be possible as surges are often thrown in, or the overall pace is of such a high quality that it's simply a case of trying to hold on.

If the athlete's aim is to run a personal best time then the task is to distribute effort as evenly as possible and to reach the finish line with the feeling that full effort has been given. In some cases that may mean that the athlete could not have maintained that pace much beyond the finish line. That is known as running oneself out. It is important to maintain a finishing effort all the way to the finish line.

Hurdle races and the steeplechase

There are several hurdle races. Younger age groups race over 75m and 80m hurdles. This progresses to 100m for women, 110m for men over high hurdles (see sequence A), 400m intermediate hurdles for men and women and 3000m steeplechase for men.

The start

In the sprint hurdles the most important part of the race to establish is the start. Eight strides are taken to the first hurdle. Even if the athlete can get there in seven it is best to take eight as the correct speed of stride is established. If the athlete is not yet strong enough to achieve eight strides then leg strength work is recommended such as step-ups, bounding and short hill sprints. To establish the belief that eight strides can be achieved the hurdles may be brought closer and, over time, gradually moved back to the correct start position. Flexibility should also be worked on to gain the maximum from each stride effort. Practice starts should always be over at least three hurdles so that the speed and rhythm of the race is being established.

64

Techniques for hurdling

Balance

Good hurdle clearance is established at take-off. The athletes should think of themselves as running on a tightrope, deviating as little as possible from the straight line to the finish. Any off-balance motion can result in loss of time. Every action should be controlled.

The lead leg

The lead leg is the leg lifted over the hurdle first. The drive over the hurdle should be initiated with a high and fast knee lift. The lower leg is held back. The foot of the lead leg has the toe up, but is not swung forward until the knee has reached its highest point. That is the point at which the heel can be driven out and then pulled down over the hurdle. From the high point the heel of the lead leg is pushed straight out, as hard as possible, just above the height of the hurdle. The heel is aimed a couple of inches to the left or right of centre depending on whether the left or right leg is the lead leg. A common fault is allowing the leg to drive towards the outside of the hurdle, or taking off so close to the hurdle that the lead leg is hooked over the hurdle.

Landing

The lead leg should be pulled down to the ground under the athlete. The hurdler should land on the ball of the

65

foot, attempting to stay as tall as possible, not allowing the knee to bend on landing. The lead leg is the landing leg and should be considered as a pivot. The hamstring is working hard to pull the body into the next stride, but if the landing position is correct the hurdler lands directly over the foot. If the landing leg is bent there can be a considerable loss of momentum.

The lead arm

For the sake of illustration take the left leg as the lead leg. The athlete's right hand and arm must balance this exaggerated knee lift. The elbow should be lifted up to shoulder height and, as the foot is driven over the top of the hurdle, the hand is extended towards that foot. Very briefly it is held out there before coming back around the trail or take-off leg. The return route of the lead arm is vital for good balance. The action is very similar to pulling water around oneself in a bath. The elbow must remain high and slightly bent (a little more than 90 degrees). The hand must be lower than the elbow and is swept around the knee. The arm being bent should prevent the hand swinging wildly behind the athlete. Straight-arm swinging often results in the hurdler going off balance for a stride or two.

The shoulders

The shoulders should be kept as square as possible. At take-off the chest should

66

lean towards the centre of the hurdle. This does not mean a torso twist, simply the lead arm is stretched out and the opposite arm is drawn back. The hand of the lead arm has the palm facing down. The other arm should be held back at approximately 90 degrees, with the palm down. The hand is held close to the body at about the level of a trouser pocket. It is then in a good position to come through in good sprint form on the follow-up stride after landing.

The trail leg

The trail leg is the one which is used to drive off the ground. That push off should be done with the greatest force possible. After take-off the toe is turned out and held up, Charlie Chaplin style. This will cause the knee to come around to the side, but the main aim should be to lift the knee up to the straight line of sprinting. The head, knee and toe should all be brought in the sprint line before the hurdler drives the foot to the ground under himself or herself for the next sprint stride.

The upper body

The upper body is bent slightly forward as the lead knee is being lifted to dive over the hurdle. That same body lean must be maintained into, over and away from the hurdle. This requires considerable abdomen strength, but it pays

67

tremendous dividends in maintaining momentum.

Where to take off

The athlete should be taking off in a position so that two thirds of the distance covered is before the hurdle and one third after, e.g. in the 110m hurdles take-off should be about 2.4m before the hurdle and landing 1.2m after. If the before and after hurdle distances are close too, say 1.8m and 1.8m, then the hurdler is coming in too close and will be 'sailing' over the hurdle. Obviously the total distance is a little less when a lower hurdle is being cleared by a younger athlete, but the point is that you can only run when you're on the ground and once you've launched into the air there is little that can be done to bring you down again. The high point of the clearance should be about 5cm before the hurdle. The athlete is literally stepping down over the hurdle.

Two hurdles

One way that the athlete can learn to push off hard is to place two hurdles one behind the next. For goodness sake don't hit them! Start with them very low and from a good footing take off.

Running between the hurdles

Hurdlers are sprinters, and therefore it is essential to work the arms between each hurdle. As in sprinting the centre of gravity should be kept high. The athletes should be running off their toes and keeping their hips high. A common error in hurdling is to see the body dip and the knees bend between hurdles and then launch an upward trajectory over the hurdle. This will result in 'floating', and the athlete must simply wait to return to the ground losing vital racing time.

Introducing hurdling action

The hurdling action can be introduced rapidly through an increasing challenge. The first aspect to establish is that the action is a driving push *out*, rather than up. This first point can be made by placing a couple of towels on the track and having the athletes long stride over them. The next step is to have some very low objects which will fall easily if knocked. Small hurdles only 9–12 inches high are ideal. They should be placed at regular intervals so that the athletes become familiar with the rhythm of hurdling. The next step is to increase the height by doubling up the mini hurdles or whatever else is being used. The main object is to allow the athletes to build up confidence in clearing a barrier without bruising a knee.

400m hurdles

As with the 100m and 110m hurdles there are a total of ten barriers in this race. In the 400m hurdles half of these

are on the bends (see sequence C). There is an advantage to leading with the left leg as the hurdler can stay on the inside of the lane. The rules of the event require the hurdler to stay within their lane and this includes the air space! This means that the left leg lead hurdler can run on the inside of the lane around the bends. The right leg lead hurdlers must clear the hurdle towards the outer part of their lane to ensure that their trail foot does not come through in the next person's lane.

Another advantage for the left leg lead hurdler is that the lean when clearing the hurdle is to the left. That means that there can be a continuation of the course around the bend. The right leg lead hurdlers briefly direct their momentum away from that curved run while clearing the barrier, and must therefore redirect their motion into the curve after landing.

Learning to lead with either leg

During the 400m hurdles fatigue creeps into the legs causing the length of stride to reduce. This makes it difficult to arrive at every barrier with the preferred lead leg. With this in mind it makes a great deal of sense to learn how to hurdle off either foot and the younger one starts that the better. Having said that, it's rarely too late to learn.

Stamina

Hurdling is physically very demanding. You are asking the body to run fast and put full effort into every clearance. With this in mind it is important that sufficient hurdling is done to ensure that there is enough specific hurdling endurance. Flat running fitness is important but not sufficient by itself. Repetition hurdle sessions should be over at least five hurdles and occasionally the hurdlers should try to run more than the total distance, e.g twelve hurdles or, for the 400m hurdler, 500m – the first 300m on the flat and the last 200m over hurdles.

Another helpful endurance hurdle session is down and back hurdling outlined in the training section for the steeplechaser. The 400m hurdler who normally runs fifteen strides between hurdles would take nine strides in the twenty yards between hurdles, the fourteen strider would take eight between and the athletes attempting thirteen strides would take seven between.

Pace judgement

In the 400m hurdles it is best to practise at the pace that you want to race, because the stride pattern will be engraved physically and mentally. As in the flat 400m there is a need to relax during a part of the race. Usually this should occur after establishing the initial speed and rhythm around the first bend. That pace can be maintained with

71

less effort down the back straight, and the term 'floating' is sometimes used to describe that fast and loose motion which allows the athlete to run without straining.

Hurdle weights

In hurdle races the correct weight placement on the base stand means that there will be an 8lb resistance to pushing the hurdle over.

Steeplechase

Depending on the age of the athlete the steeplechase event is over 1500m, 2000m or 3000m. The first and last of these equate in terms of times to the athlete's mile and two-mile flat times. The 1500m includes thirteen hurdles and three water jumps. The 2000m has eighteen hurdles and five water jumps. The 3000m event has twenty-eight hurdles and seven water jumps. The water jump is not included in the first lap.

Steeplechase barriers

Steeplechase barriers are three feet high and solid. The hurdling action for steeplechasers should be as similar to intermediate hurdling as possible, with the exception of the water jump. Hurdlers have to practise for many hours to create the awareness of how to adjust their stride when approaching each hurdle. The problem is magnified for the steeplechaser; the approach is more variable. Other athletes are often in the same path, partially obscuring a clear view of the barrier. Furthermore, the water jump is not simply a hurdle.

Water jump clearance

Arguably this is the most important part of the race as a poor clearance each time here is very tiring. Twelve feet (3.7m) of water extends beyond the base of the landing side. In order to establish a rhythm and a reliable stride pattern into the water barrier some athletes place a check mark at the side of the track seven or eight strides from take-off.

The most common type of water jump clearance is for the athlete to run at the barrier placing the heel and instep of the

The Polish steeplechaser, Maminski. If, when taking the water jump, the back part of the instep strikes the top of the barrier, the toe may be used to push off from the front edge. The body stays low over the barrier and the athlete usually lands within a foot of the edge of the water

73

b

d

lead leg on top of it. The lead leg knee remains flexed as the athlete crosses the barrier, keeping the body low. Once the body is beyond the barrier the leg in contact with it is extended and the runner pushes out. The thigh of the landing leg is lifted, as if approaching a

c

e

new hurdle, then the leg extended in a long step towards the far end of the water. The depth diminishes from a metre directly under the barrier sloping up to ground level twelve feet (3.7m) beyond the barrier. Most steeplechasers land about half a metre from the end of

f

the water. Their follow-up stride should be well onto the flat part of the track, beyond the water. In order to do that the knee of the push-off leg should be brought through high and into the running line, again as in good hurdling form. Another advantage of this action is that only one foot will be wet throughout the race.

I have used the 'lead leg' to refer here to the leg lifted up onto the barrier. Most steeplechasers prefer that at the water jump the lead leg be the normal take-off foot for hurdling. This allows them to have the stronger push-off leg driving from the top of the barrier and the normal hurdle landing foot to land on.

Body lean and arm action

As in hurdle clearance the body lean should be maintained throughout the water jump clearance. When driving out

76

from the top of the water jump barrier, the arm motion must be exaggerated to balance the lifted knee. One arm is lifted and extended when the lead leg is lifted towards the barrier, then the other arm motion is exaggerated when the opposite knee is driven out across the water.

Tactics and pace judgement

Tactics and pace judgement for the steeplechaser are similar to those described in the section on middle- and long-distance running. The biggest difference is that the steady flow which a middle-distance runner enjoys is constantly being interrupted by the barrier in steeplechasing.

Positioning coming into each barrier

If the competitor does not know the hurdling capability of his opponents then there is a great deal of sense in staying out of harm's way at the early barriers. A good hurdler will be able to pick up a metre or more into, over and away from each barrier. If you are a decent hurdler, and are approaching a barrier behind a poor hurdler, there could be difficulty. If he is stutter-stepping or slowing his momentum on landing, there is a problem of either running up his back or having your own momentum severely interrupted. The expenditure of effort in constantly stop-

77

ping and restarting will greatly add to the tiredness factor. In summary, it makes sense to try to get a clear run into each hurdle. Doing that will also enable the chaser to accelerate slightly into each barrier. This is important to maintain good hurdling form.

Training

Similar to the special needs of the 400m hurdler, the steeplechaser must include a great deal of hurdling in his schedule. With five barriers per 400m in the race, there is every reason to incorporate hurdling into several sessions each week. It makes sense to work at close to race pace to establish the physical and mental patterning required for sighting and clearing the barriers at the proper speed. Interval training over the barriers would produce this desired effect. I would recommend that the steeplechaser devotes some time to practice over slightly higher hurdles on the straight. This is a similar strategy to running over-distance for strength. If the chaser can develop reasonable technique over higher hurdles then he has an advantage as the race develops. As hurdling becomes more of an effort, reasonable clearances will be more easily achieved and maintained.

A useful multiple hurdle session is accomplished by placing hurdles on every other high hurdle marking, setting the hurdles at normal barrier height

78

(three feet), facing down in one lane and back in the opposite direction. The athlete runs one length, circles at the far end and returns. This down and back running can be repeated on a continuous running basis for two, three or more loops, producing a tough endurance hurdle workout. The turn around can be chosen anywhere, but with a 15-yard run in and 20 yards between, four hurdles gives about a 90-yard run in each direction. Eight strides would be used to the first hurdle. If practice is being given to alternating the lead leg then eight or ten strides between hurdles would be used. Nine strides would be the normal pattern between hurdles for the average adult male – the landing step is not counted, i.e. the follow-up step is counted as one. It will be discovered that multiple hurdling requires considerable strength and endurance.

Race walking

School-age children may compete over 1600m, 3000m or 5000m. Junior Internationals are held over 10km with Olympic competition over 20km (almost 12 miles) and 50km (more than 30 miles).

Rules

There are two rules which distinguish walking from running. The first is that the athlete must, at all times, have one foot in contact with the ground. That means that the heel of the advanced foot must be in contact with the ground before the toe of the pushing foot leaves the ground. The second rule is that the support leg must be straight as it comes under the body. Violation of the first rule is called 'lifting' and the second is referred to as 'creeping'.

Technique

The simplest way of discovering the way to race walk is to begin walking normally and gradually increase the pace. Athletes will soon discover that their arms come up and swing across the body, with the elbow bent at about 90 degrees. They will also discover that in

80

order to remain flowing rather than stiff and jerky in their motion they will have to relax and let their hips rotate a little on each stride. This enables the stride to be longer and more fluid. At first only little effort seems necessary, but the demands quickly become apparent.

The walker should remain virtually upright or with the slightest forward lean. Any pronounced forward or backward lean produces poor technique and reduces speed.

Foot placement should be in a direct line, one following the next. As in sprinting the outside of the foot goes down first, but in the case of the walker the heel strikes the ground first with the toe still up at about a 45-degree angle.

Training requirements

Walking is primarily an endurance event, but the requirements also place stress on overall conditioning. Because of the hip rotation the abdomen must be well conditioned. The arms are far more powerfully used than in running events, therefore weight training has added importance. Flexibility work is as essential as for runners; it will reduce injury and allow the walker to get the most from each stride. However the most important ingredient is, inevitably, walking.

Specific training

It is estimated that 90 per cent of the build-up phase should be long walks.

Ian McCombie, during a record-breaking
performance, demonstrates the
requirements for race walking. The heel of

the leading leg must touch the ground
before the driving foot has left the ground,
and the leg is drawn unbent under the body

The pace should be varied as with distance running, from slow and easy, through fartlek to relatively fast. Once each week a very long walk is used by the mature walker. This should not be included by the developing youngster. As pointed out in different sections, the aim for young athletes is to learn the basics and enjoy their sport. Intense and prolonged training by those under about fifteen can lead to serious structural problems in later life.

Two other forms of training are considered beneficial, but with some reservation. Both running and cross-country skiing have definite endurance and strength benefits, but neither mirror the requirements of walking. The basic principles and format which apply to running training apply equally to race walking.

The mental side of training

I cannot allow even an introductory book to leave out mention of the mental side of training. Up until the 1980s coaches were concerned primarily with technical proficiency and physical preparation. Even if you have those two aspects fully covered, the third element of the triangle is vital: namely what the athlete decides to do. Every individual has to make decisions all day long. Shall I get up? What shall I have to eat? Shall I train today? Do I really want to push myself in training? Do I have to finish the number of repetitions set?

The point being made is that we totally control what we do physically by making mental decisions. Often we're not even conscious of it. In order to achieve one must become conscious of choice, and make the decisions which best fit in with what is really wanted.

Goal-setting

Realistic goal-setting is the most fundamental and vital part of mental training. Goals set too high, as with the perfectionist, are doomed to failure; goals set too low produce no motivation

because there is no challenge. A goal must therefore be a good challenge one that can be mastered in a specific time-frame. Goals must be constantly reviewed and renewed.

Visualization

In my study of sport's highest achievers* I discovered that 80 per cent used mental rehearsal and imagery as a highly valued part of their preparation for competition. These athletes spent some of their quiet time thinking about themselves in the forthcoming competitive situation. They tried to create the most detailed sense of the experience. They imagined themselves, physically, in their event at competition time.

Try to rehearse the best possible performance under a wide variety of situations. Steve Cram said that he likes to imagine how each of his top opponents might run the race. He comes up with four or five options of how the race might go. He then imagines how he would best compete within each of those possibilities.

The idea is to rehearse mentally the

*Should you wish to read more of the experiences of those who held together best under top competition, my book on sport's highest achievers is called The Pursuit of Sporting Excellence (Collins, 1986). Additionally, a superb practical guide to mental training has been produced by Chris Connolly and John Syer called Sporting Body Sporting Mind (Cambridge University Press, 1984).

most positive performance that the individual can expect of themselves. Daley Thompson spends the last couple of days before every major competition going through every event mentally. He sometimes imagines himself under the greatest possible pressure, having failed twice at the opening height in either the high jump or the pole vault. He mentally handles that anxiety and sees himself successfully clearing that height. This happened to him in the pole vault in the 1984 Olympics and in the high jump in the 1986 Commonwealth Games.

Imagery is another form of mental control. The athlete discovers a mental image which will help lower or raise pressure in the non-competitive or pre-competitive situation. The Soviet sprinter Valeriy Borzov spoke of mentally finding a place to relax, possibly alone beside a stream in a forest. He would switch to that quiet scene when wanting to relax before a heat in a major games. The Irish hammer thrower Pat O'Callaghan used flags in practice, set at the distances of his closest rivals. This was his way of challenging himself, creating competition and focusing his concentration. The interesting thing was that he used the image of the field to lower his anxiety when in competition. When the presence of the opposition was playing on his nerves he imagined the field, and thought all I have to do is throw beyond the flags!

A word to coaches and parents

When a coach or parent is starting out with youngsters there should be a clear perspective, namely that they are there to *help*. Trouble comes when the coach or parent is trying to live through the athlete. There's a very fine line between being pleased with the athlete's successes, and wanting the youngster to improve because it will advance the status or prestige of the coach or parent. One check is to assess whether there is as much concern being shown for the athlete, as a person, off the field as there is for the results on it.

One question which should be asked is what is the reason for wanting the athlete to improve. Here the coach is being asked to retain the bigger picture. By the time athletes have finished many years of endeavour they should be able to reflect that they have learned a lot more about themselves and life through their participation in sport. Results are important, but any acclaim or medals are a bonus. The athlete should be able to look back, each week, and feel that the experience has been enjoyable and intrinsically worthwhile.

Most coaches will have had the benefit of that experience. They will know that in each season the athlete will deal with health and sickness; athletes will flow with strength and be stopped by injury; they will face excitement in winning and disappointment through losing, joy in establishing a personal best and frustration through not doing so. There are many more facets, but the point being made is that the experiences are there from which to learn. Does an injured athlete lose the attention of the coach? It ought to be a time to look at the possible causes of the injury. Could the athlete work on developing more strength in the area of a muscle pull? While recovering from a turned ankle could the arm strength be improved? Is the athlete going to be beaten by setbacks or toughened in his or her resolve to show what he or she is really made of? This is where the help of a coach or parent is so important.

In every coach-athlete relationship there is a need for co-operation, mutual respect and encouragement. The coach assists the athlete to gain in competence and confidence. Hopefully athletes become better balanced, physically and socially. From their sport they should learn greater self-discipline and better use of time. They should discover that, to a large extent, they control how much they can improve; there can be a helpful carry over to what they do with the rest of their lives.

Athletes need support and encouragement to fulfil their talent. They do best with a stable, consistent upbring-

ing. The coach guides the athlete, concentrating on personal improvement as much as winning. The aim may be to win but not all have that ability, and there is always someone ready to knock the champion off the top. Competing well is a challenge, and competitive athletes put pressure on themselves to do well. The coach can assist by keeping the experience enjoyable for both of them.

The inner game approach

One way in which coaches can remain fresh, no matter how many years they are involved in coaching, is to follow the methods of coaching outlined in *The Inner Game**. The author, Tim Gallwey, examines many important aspects of the internal and mental states of the successful athlete. He realized that all humans have an immense capacity to learn but often cause their own mental blocks. The body taught itself how to walk and how to talk. Yet we don't trust it to learn sport without giving it a lot of instruction. Gallwey suggests that the coach should be less directive about technique than he is about the athlete's focus of attention. By focusing on the

Should you wish to know more about The Inner Game *either read the book by Tim Gallwey, and/or contact Alan Fine, Inside Out Training, Penny Hill Park Country Club, College Ride, Bagshot, Surrey, GU19 5ET. Tel. 0276 76400.*

sensation of a technique or action, the body will automatically correct itself to become more fluid. The hardest thing for the coach and athlete to do is not force the correction. The conscious mind wants to take control. However, the conscious mind doesn't know which muscles to adjust to make the best movement correction.

Coaches usually try to correct an action by telling the athlete what they are doing wrong and telling them how to correct the fault. The inner game method is for the coach to help the athlete discover how to correct the fault by asking them questions which raise their perception in an area or areas where the coach or athlete see a need for change.

For example, when coaching a female hurdler, I saw that she was rather stiff and upright when going over the hurdles. I asked her to put her focus on her upper body and assess a number between one and ten – one being parallel with the ground and ten completely erect. I asked her to run over the hurdles again and sense what number her upper half felt like. She came back with eight and a half. I asked her to experiment with how it felt at different numbers. I also asked her to picture the world record holder and to see what number she would be on if she ran like her?

With this type of approach, the experience for the athlete is one of self-

discovery. The object is increased personal awareness which leads to improved technique. The female athlete mentioned moved from the rather stiff upright upper body position to feeling much faster and more comfortable, coming away from the hurdle with her upper half holding a far more effective forward lean. Her learning was from her own experience, rather than just from instruction, and it is therefore more probable that she will retain the improved action. It also means that the athlete is sharing responsibility for her learning.

The inner game method may take slightly longer, but the learning is more personal and permanent. After all, what is needed is to have the improved motion become second nature. Under pressure we all revert to what is 'second nature', and if the fundamentals are not sound then under competitive pressure poor technique will let the athlete down.

My very best wishes to each athlete who is endeavouring to improve. It is a long-term quest in one of the most demanding sports, and I hope you will find this book of some assistance.